A Book of Love

verses for men in appreciation of women

A Book of Love

verses for men in appreciation of women

by

Alexander George

ISBN: 1-58721-982-4

1stBooks - rev. 6/13/00

About The Book

Okay, the title is pretentious, from the 1958 Doo Wop hit by the Monotones. Old enough to remember? *"Well I wonder wonder who baaduubaa who, who wrote the Book of Love!?"* The song never does answer the question, and as regards who wrote *this* Book of Love, I'm afraid I can't either. The voice is only partly mine; the rest "came through me", or in other words, was channeled. I don't know the identity of that other voice, but I assure you there were no 360° spinning heads or ectoplasmic streamers involved in the creative process. The poems are not my personal expression; they are more universal. They present a spiritualized vision of love between man and woman. Although most of the poems are addressed to men, there is much for women and for couples to appreciate. If you're a guy reading this, I hope they will speak to you, resonate some insight in yourself. I know I could have benefited from some brotherly advice, some guidance in my relations with women. Maybe you won't have to screw up as badly as I did. As for a book of appreciation of men, that is better left to a woman to write.

The writing happened in a conducive setting, the tropical country of Brazil, home to some of the world's most beautiful women. Love, romance and spirituality are in the air. (Some say it's in the water.) The culture, including the language, Portuguese, seems to bring out the sensual in everyone. The most frequently heard words in popular songs are *saudades* (longing) *coração* (heart), *paixão* (passion) and of course, *amor*.

Is this poetry, free verse, or just some prose divided up into lines? You decide. Whatever it is, I have arranged it into sections, almost as a cycle or a story, but it was not written with that intention or in the order in which the pieces appear. The sections--appreciating women, seeing women, new love, love-making and relationship--are meant neither to be definitive nor exhaustive of each topic.

In this generation it would seem the torch of progress is passing on to women. They are wise and beautiful, living extraordinary lives, cutting a path for others to emulate. It is for us men to grant women the stage, to step aside and honor and empower them for the many blessings they bring.

A.G. São Paulo April, 2000

for Cristiane

Invocation to Women

Gladden our eyes
with your unspeakable beauty.
Teach our hearts.
Show us God's grace and wisdom
that we may discover them in ourselves.
Daughters, sisters, mothers, mates,
carry the seeds of our species,
accompany us hand in hand
through our growing.
Receive us that we may cherish and serve you,
on this world and in Paradise,
from now unto eternity.

First Lines

Appreciating Women

Seeing Women

New Love

Love Making

Relationship

Appreciating Women

Woman is man's complement,
his compass to point him toward his heart.
Woman is that which man
must bring forth within himself.
Alone, men lose their way,
blind to their guides surrounding them,
demonstrating the way in everyday devotions.
How else shall we find
the gates of Heaven,
except hand in hand,
man and woman?

She walks in grace,
fully conscious of the treasure she is.
Yes, she has cared for herself
to offer a form of sensual delight
to draw your fickle eye,
your childish heart.
All this of her that is visible,
but bait on her shimmering surface,
by which she will lead you to the depths,
where she dwells in beauty,
consecrated to love.

A banquet is before you.
You hunger, but for what?
Will you partake only of her form,
her scents and sounds, her delectable movements?
A woman is intangible, a being of love.
She cannot be seen, only felt.
Return to yourself;
from your depth you will find her.
When your struggle to be in your heart is victorious,
she will meet you there effortlessly.
All that you may learn of love in this life,
she already is.

The young woman is a flower;
allow her imperfections
even as her sweet nectar grants you new youth,
as her lifespring overflows
into the cavities of your soul.
Forgive the occasional thorn,
the rough undersurface of a leaf;
the soil that fed her beginnings was diseased,
the gardeners trod unknowingly
upon her growth.
Firm is her skin, taut over a life essence
that would burst forth.
It is for you to unlock the fragrance.
In your gentleness, her hardness dissolves;
new blossoms bow to you in gratitude and joy.

The woman of prime
is a well of experience,
a fruit at the peak of ripeness,
full of sweetness from life's seasons,
yearning to be plucked and eaten,
to shudder in fulfillment
long dreamed of,
long desired;
this is the woman of prime.
Her eternal youth all the more clearly visible
at the onset of age.
Her timeless perfection flawless
against the marks of time.
No deeper gratitude than hers,
when her beauty is seen and savored;
she knows each love
could be the last.

Her features record an entire life:
the virtues, the excesses,
the wisdom, the folly,
the victories, the little deaths,
the light and the dark
all play across her face.
Know that what she did
she did for love,
in search of love,
and in the pain of its absence.
When the worn envelop falls away,
when the web is unwoven,
all the twistings will unwind,
the fears will dissolve into peace
and the heaviness lighten.
Only the beautiful will remain;
a soul will stand in purity
one step closer to its Maker.

Missing the sweetness of life?
Needing woman to be sweet?
Oh, indeed she is,
exquisitely so,
but if that is all you seek,
you will miss her.
She is not candy to be unwrapped,
tasted and consumed.
A woman is real and true,
with dimensions and facets
like a cut diamond.
She is not an idea in your mind,
but a full-blooded human,
the very complement of your being,
your equal in every way.
She is free-willed, unpredictable,
and impossible to control.
See her not as possession, but as partner;
not the proviant for the journey, but the fellow traveler.
Yes, it is intended that she refresh you,
but with her evolving mind, heart and soul.
As sweet as woman is,
her source and your source is yet sweeter.
Satisfy your sweet tooth at source
and rejoice in the fullness of woman.

Seeing Women

Do you see only women?
Are men invisible to you?
Are you one who ignores men,
turning away from your brother,
seeking solace only with the sisters?
Do not burden women with your emptiness
from lack of loving contact with men.
Bring the women in your life the fullness
of a heart that loves men.

What beauty,
but so coldly she turns away!
If she will not meet your eyes in joy,
step back with respect.
Can you not feel the wound in her being?
Violated by a thousand staring eyes,
turning aside a daily onslaught,
while longing to be truly seen,
longing to give herself.

Stand in her shoes for a moment.
Do not demand her eyes;
only empathy is appropriate in her presence.
Only if she calls you to her
may you approach.
She will give you a sign.
You will know.

Look at her, my brother,
but don't let her notice.
Do you see how she contains herself?
Do you wonder why?
Her passion is great;
it has always been so,
but she will not let it flow.
Like a river rising behind a dam,
her passion has no outlet.
At your touch this dam may crumble,
and you will find yourself tumbling
in the most amazing white waters.

Can you tell she does not love herself?
She thinks herself plain and undesirable.
Do you agree?
No, don't.
If you can convince her of her truth,
her beauty will be released and overwhelm you.
Feel her hands! How delicate their touch!
See her eyes animate with delight!
Taste the hunger and eloquence of her mouth!
Hear her secret voice of murmurs and sighs!
As her body comes alive,
honor her sacred dance of self
and celebrate who she really is.
Finally, do not omit to nurture her heart
with your gratitude,
for you are in her debt.

In the hollow reality you inhabit,
your attune your eye to the beauty that is woman.
Beside her face and figure even nature pales,
fit only to be a backdrop, a mere frame.
A point of light and grace,
she preserves somehow
a heart sweet with love
amidst the disillusionment of experience.
As you scan across the temporal wasteland,
she appears as the remedy to your sickness of soul.
Your eye remains and feeds in longing,
hoping to recapture what was lost,
conceiving of what could be.
Yes, delight in her unique beauty,
how her features and body reflect the inner person,
one of an infinite procession
issuing from the Creator's fount.
But you will never understand woman
until you understand yourself.
Know that she is your mirror and have faith
such beauty exists within you.
Turn your vision inward
and begin the long journey to core
where you heal yourself
and come to love yourself.
Only thus will your world re-animate,
to become a place of color, life and joy,
as it was in your innocence.

New Love

You close your eyes.
A fruit appears before you,
and you realize you have dreamt of it.
A hand becomes visible
cradling the fruit;
then an arm, and the body of a woman.
She, too, is of a dream.
Approaching you, presenting the fruit
in which there is no fault,
she turns it before your eyes.
Perfectly ripe, a rainbow-colored skin,
she passes it close to your face;
its aroma is sweet and fresh.
She presses it against your cheek;
its skin is smooth and warm.
She rests it in your hand,
a body firm and succulent,
without fault.
As she begins to peel the fruit,
your eyes open.
Now realize who she is
and what she offers.

She appreciates little things;
a word,
a gesture,
a look,
a thoughtfulness
could speak to her,
convince her,
be the sign she awaits

that turns the key
that unlocks her heart.

Who knows which it will be?
A mystery.

Reveal yourself to her in the little things,
that she may know you love her.

She has fallen silent;
do not speak.
Her eyes search for yours;
do not glance aside.
All that you may aspire to
is as close as the hand squeezing yours.
All that sleeps hidden within you
is vividly awake before you,
reaching toward you.
Her eyes offer you a glimpse of yourself.
You have only to recognize the gift
to receive it.

You are waiting for the first kiss.
Her lips are all you can think of.
Your chest aches to press against her heart.
Patience.
She is an artist of love.
Give her time to create.
She is guiding your intimacy,
initiating each tiny increment
at the right moment
as soon as she is ready
so it can be savored,
for more beauty,
for more excitement.
Her eyes tempt and tease;
what will she do next?
Lucky man…

Before her there was nothing.
You cannot remember who you were
or how you felt.
After knowing her one week
you know only that you are happy.
A dark veil has lifted and you are simpler,
getting deeper into yourself.
All the signs you asked for have been given.
You are hers, and she is yours.
Time to start believing in life again.

"I am waves," she utters in innocence,
poised next to you on the grass.
Suddenly she moves;
her lips, her body surge to you;
mouth to mouth, she envelops you,
driving you backwards,
demanding you again and again.
You cannot think,
you do not want to think.
You know only that she is your destiny.
You resonate in waves with her
and return to life.

Your new love perplexes you one day:
"I have something to tell you," she says.
"Do you know what?"
What does she mean, you wonder.
In the night you awaken next to her.
She awakens with you and comes closer.
Her head rolls toward you,
her mouth is against your ear.
"I am going to tell you the thing I said I would."
She is speaking slowly;
her voice is barely audible,
but it reaches into your heart.
"I love you."

You were becalmed in sterile seas,
fading into stagnant waters,
presiding alone over the death of your soul.
At her approach your flimsy vessel shuddered and sank,
the waves of her love seized and disoriented you.
Now you are lost in waters warm and melting,
in currents unfamiliar.
She appears as a brilliant-eyed serpent,
a goddess of desire,
coiling high above you,
ready to strike at your invitation,
ready to carry you to your fate,
to your depths,
where you will drown
and begin life anew.

You dreamt of being with her and now that you are,
the reality of your togetherness surpasses the dream.
Her presence fills and thrills you;
in the magic of lovemaking she incandesces,
and your thirst for beauty is slaked.
But in the illusion of your incompleteness,
it arises again and again,
and to your shame,
you cast a critical eye upon her.
From this angle, in that mundane moment,
you miss the splendor of form and light you know she can be.
My friend, why must she be perfect?
May she not be human, a woman,
as flawed and fluctuating as yourself?
She cares little how you appear;
she measures your heart.
A man may not presume to measure
the heart of the one who teaches him love;
he may only reverence the gift.

Love Making

Behold the lovers;
witness the primordial rite
of flesh seeking flesh,
the divinely ordained nature
of man and woman created together
to be together.
Only in each others arms
would we know freedom.
Skin attuned to skin, we truly feel;
eyes meeting eyes, we perceive the soul;
heart pressed to heart
in release of love,
a light bursting forth
from the living clay.
The triumph of love
as a transcendent fragrance
arising from the instinctual fires;
and heaven descends to earth
in answer to the biological children
of time and space
who dare to live love.

Why let your wave dash alone upon the shore,
when together you could be the ocean?
Will your soul ever be satisfied
so long as your own pleasure is the more important?
Have you dedicated yourself to a fellow voyager,
even if for but a single night?
Have you attuned to her need,
sensing what would fill her heart this night?
Have you come empty-handed or bearing a gift?
The angels find no fault in generosity.
Seeking the higher pleasure you are edified.

How long has this being lived without touch?
She who was born to love,
to share her delight,
to open hearts...
What tragedy, what waste!
Now in your arms she balances,
trembling in surrender,
her body re-activates,
flashes at warp speed
across the months and years
of want and denial.
How she melts into you!
Could you ever give yourself so fully?
Even now as she reawakens
she is a revelation;
she teaches you more
than you can encompass.
In gratitude, do not part
without assisting her out of the maze.
Together, roll the stone
of insight across the entrance,
that she may never again wander
in such painful longing,
in search of dubious lessons.

The most beautiful place on earth is the heart of woman.
Kiss the middle of her chest where beats her heart,
where womankind keeps love alive on earth.
Stroke this place with reverence.
Kiss her breasts as you would her heart.
Lay your head worshipfully between them
to hear the very rhythm of life.

The woman who loves not her own body,
who entertains discontent and shame,
disappears as you pull her hips greedily to you.
Caress her hips with desire.
Embrace them, remind them of all they are,
the epitome of all that is full and round,
fertile with life, the very center of things.
Partake of the fullness that eludes you
in your thin life.

Do you know how to hold a woman?
Let her nestle in safety at your side;
your chest is the natural resting place for her head.
Let her find refuge in your arms;
for a soul that above all else values love,
existence on this troubled planet is wearying.
Give her your strength;
infuse her with the power of you.
Feed her precious heart
that it may stay open and feeling,
nurturing all with its wisdom and affection.

You believe yourself to be holding her,
but it is she who holds you.
She has no need of powerful arms;
it is her love that embraces you
and gives you sanctuary
that will never confine or diminish you,
that will only add onto you
and set you free.

As you hold her
keep looking in her eyes,
keep appreciating who she is.
Let this be your anchor,
lest you become lost
in the beguiling
but lesser realm of sensation.
Return always to the higher reality of personality contact,
of communion between the God created
elements of being in her and in yourself.
And in the fullness of heart she inspires in you
close your eyes to recognize this beauty as your own.
Then return your eyes to hers in gratitude.

She has admitted you to the most sensitive,
most vulnerable part of her.
You move gently, drinking in her reactions.
There is no sweeter moment;
you know you live for this.
Her pleasure and surrender blend
to a degree you can never know,
only witness with awe.
You let her pace be your pace;
she has time to savor each thrust.
And now you pause, interrupting the rhythm,
and a tiny doubt enters her mind.
And now you slide deeper
and remain as her pleasure swells.
Swiftly and surely, before you realize,
her beauty has enveloped you.
You love here more and more.

You sense something wrong.

She grows still beneath you.

She is withdrawing.

She is gone and you are alone.

You wait next to her.

Her closed eyes fill with tears.

When she speaks,
listen, for what she says
she has never spoken aloud.

This is your test:
how unconditional is your love?

Her sighs in your ear blend with the pines soughing above,
and you remember the waterfall you passed earlier;
bathing together in the torrent,
it anointed you with just such a sound,
and like the water released into the void,
so is she is now in your arms.

Listen again as her breath comes and goes
and hear the poplar leaves rustling in the invisible breeze.
She trembles and disappears
to join wind and water,
and there issues from her the universal sound,
the sound of creation,
the sound of life
and of death;
the death of wave on sand,
of forest in flame.
With head arched back,
she allows you to consume her;
she dies and is reborn.

She lies still as a mountain lake.
Your shafts of sunlight warm and illumine her sublime depths;
her pliant waters ripple into motion
across the surface of the bed.

Her currents come alive,
seeking direction, seeking outlet.
She swells up toward you suddenly;
her mouth is moist and deep,
joining with yours insistently,
drawing you down into her.

She flows like a river in your arms,
her force is barely contained within the banks of her body.
Your light guides her accelerating current,
as it sweeps past every boulder, every obstacle toward release.

She is the rounded mass of water
that bulges into space at the head of a cascade,
taking you with her
suspended for an indelible moment,
eyes looking into eyes,
then falling, falling, into white water ecstasy.

She rests and meanders to the peaceful sea,
taking you with her,
and in her arms you have no fear
of the salt air, the sound of waves
and the vast horizon welcoming you home.

Relationship

Do not make a prison of relationship;
trust your partner and allow her freedom.
Take that risk.
Own your needs and fears
and follow them to their source within you.
Do not attempt to slake them in her.
Let her breathe, and let yourself breathe.
Even as you need love,
you are love, you are complete.
You are that which you seek.
The real world is a world of love,
but it is also a world of freedom.
Enter the real world together.

Guard the place in your heart that is your love's
and admit no stranger there.
What you have given her is for no other.
As the forbidden fruit is the sweeter, however,
allow your imagination freedom.
But never fail to bring your passion home!
It's absence, like the stranger's presence,
will be noted immediately.

The world is full of beautiful women.
Would you posses them all and have none?
Would you have a new woman each night,
but none to share your days?
Would you ransom your heart away
to each enchanting smile and exciting figure,
one after the other in endless succession,
variations of the same fantasy?
Are you caught in the spell,
adrift in the sea of yin?
How strong the biological urges are,
but you were not born to be enslaved.
Your challenge as a man is to overcome instinct,
to attain to higher appreciations.
Rise above the earthly currents within your psyche,
and build a sense of self on solid ground,
not on approval or prowess.
The feminine you seek outside you
is alive within you.
Love, youth and passion
you will only find through self-renewal.

Communicate,
for there are no secrets in the universe;
what you would conceal you reveal.
What should have been said
fills the silences between you
and widens them
until a chasm opens up
and you are no longer of one mind.
A note of discord reverberates subliminally,
that is felt,
that confuses.

Betray another and you can never
again be close until it is admitted.
The unspoken confession is a lie that saddens your soul,
that will taint all that you share, ever after.
Love and truth do not coexist with guilt and deceit.
Truly, that single step off the path
leaves you tumbling into the abyss.
Think well before sacrificing the integrity of relationship,
for what remains is
no longer real.
Communicate.

Can the ground of your existence
not be a part of you?
Can the center your life
lie beyond the circumference of your being?
A human relationship is a place of dreams,
but it cannot contain your destiny.
It can never be primary,
only secondary.
A relation with another being
cannot be the fount of your life;
this is found within you,
and no other relation can ever take its place.

Do you demand of her
more than you demand of yourself?
Can your outer life
be other than your inner life?
Relation can be no more than you are.
It cannot make you happy;
you make you happy.
Self realization is the capital you bring to relation.
Work out your internal equations
to solve those external riddles.
Clear some land
before attempting to erect that castle.

Does your love disappoint you?
Are you drifting away?
Don't wait for her to happen;
lead the way!
What you want to experience with her,
become!
Be free
that she might desire to grow wings
to soar at your side.
Feel
so it is safe for her to feel,
to be real with you.
Listen and communicate
to inspire her to be present
and share all of herself.
Desire
to encourage her sleeping sensuality
to awaken and play.
Love
to be worthy of her,
so her love can flow to you.

Love the woman
who walks by your side, holding your hand,
who without thinking, caresses you,
who prepares a meal with no sense of obligation,
who gives you all her attention when you speak,
who supports you in adversity,
who wants the good for you,
who surrenders herself in love,
who misses you in your absence,
who has moods,
who loses her temper,
who thinks for herself,
who has attractions to other men,
who has character faults,
whose body is aging.
Love the mirror of you she is.
Love yourself through her.
Love the woman.

Be a team in love.
Stand shoulder to shoulder
and share a vision,
facing the challenge of living as one.
Be against no one and nothing;
be for Truth, Goodness, and Beauty.
Make not an island of your togetherness,
rather stay connected to the rest of humanity.
Offer the spirit of your love to the world.

About the Author

Dance is the love of my life. I fell in love with ballet at age 15 in San Diego, where my mother was doing her best to raise me and my two brothers after divorcing my dad. Two years later I took off to New York City to study ballet on scholarship at the Harkness House. I wasn't too well behaved, so got kicked out of there and passed through other schools, getting married in the meantime at the ripe old age of 21. New York was a tough place for an adolescent to grow up, but it sure was interesting in the late 60's. Saw a lot of dance and starting performing in small modern groups and with the New York City Opera as a Joffrey School trainee. Got initiated into Transcendental Meditation and followed the Indian master, Meher Baba. Got exposed to the Primal Scream by Arthur Janov and went into a tailspin depression. A few years later I did that therapy in Norway under the care of Lois Schwarz. Before that I had danced with the National Ballet of Canada and the Norwegian National Ballet. My career was going gangbusters with the Cullberg Ballet in Stockholm, but I was a mess after my wife and I separated. That's when I entered therapy. Saved my life. I moved back to the States and began teaching ballet with the California Ballet Company in San Diego, at the same time beginning the study of massage. For a while I was doing both, teaching for various groups in the city and also doing holistic bodywork. I had two periods away, one in Germany and another in Israel, teaching ballet for professional companies and schools.

I moved to Harbin Hot Springs in northern California just after turning forty. Wanted to experience community. It was a dream and a nightmare. My creativity could really blossom, but personality conflicts over the years were painful. At Harbin I became involved in aquatic bodywork, first as a practitioner, then as an innovator and teacher. And that's what I've been doing for the last ten years. I had a gift for writing since a teenager, but didn't do much with it. Check out my website, aquaticwritings.com for the articles I've written as a teacher of the water work. As a dancer on stage and doing free dance I had many times experienced the phenomenon of channeling, feeling that the movement came through me, rather than from me. I learned to channel verbally from my friend, Mary-el, at Harbin Hot Springs and began to incorporate that degree of inspiration into my teaching. I'm a Virgo, so service is important to me. I believe each of us has a life purpose that has a social dimension. I fancy that I contribute to the awakening of the planet. I like to be a part of healing and nurturing. I like to inspire. The challenge is to keep embodying the noble ideas that come through.

It was at Harbin that I began to know people better. I had many friendships and acquaintances. Though not a Solomon or Joe Namath, I have shared intimacy with many women in relationship and encounter. These experiences form the background for the poetry. I am completely in love with the feminine spirit.

www.ingramcontent.com/pod-product-compliance
Ingram Content Group UK Ltd.
Pitfield, Milton Keynes, MK11 3LW, UK
UKHW040017200726
13854UKWH00001B/245